BUILDING
BLOCKS
___
SCIENCE

ANIMAL STRUCTURE AND CLASSIFICATION

JOSEPH MIDTHUN   SAMUEL HITI

WORLD
BOOK

www.worldbook.com

World Book, Inc.
180 North LaSalle Street
Suite 900
Chicago, Illinois 60601
USA

For information about other World Book publications,
visit our website at www.worldbook.com
or call 1-800-WORLDBK (967-5325).
For information about sales to schools and libraries,
call 1-800-975-3250 (United States),
or 1-800-837-5365 (Canada).

Building Blocks of Science:
  Animal Structure and Classification
ISBN: 978-0-7166-7878-6 (trade, hc.)
ISBN: 978-0-7166-7886-1 (pbk.)
ISBN: 978-0-7166-2961-0 (e-book, EPUB3)

Acknowledgments:
Created by Samuel Hiti and Joseph Midthun
Art by Samuel Hiti
Text by Joseph Midthun
Special thanks to Syril McNally

TABLE OF CONTENTS

There is a glossary on page 30. Terms defined in the glossary
are in type **that looks like this** on their first appearance.

Animals are **organisms**.

Living things!

You can find animals moving all across Earth.

They travel the forests, the plains, the skies—in towns and cities and the country, too.

All animals have certain body parts, called **structures,** in common...

...and animals come in all different shapes and sizes.

HOO?

Almost all animals move by themselves...

FLAP
FLAP
FLAP

SHRSTK

...they need to move to drink water, eat food, and find shelter.

crack

munch munch

Sound familiar?

It should!

Since, you're a member of the **animal kingdom,** too!

ANIMAL BODIES

Scientists have named over one million animals living on Earth, but there could be as many as 50 million kinds of animals alive today!

Since there are so many types of animals, their body structures, or parts, are different from one another.

But, all animal bodies have many structures that do certain jobs.

From **cells** to **organ systems** to appearance, structures can help you identify an animal.

Most animals have some kind of body part to help them move around.

Some have arms or legs.

Some have fins to flip—

—or wings to flap.

Feathers are structures that help birds fly.

Feathers also keep birds warm.

wwssh

wwssh

wssh

Mammals have fur or hair to help keep warm.

By observing their different structures, all animals can be studied and classified.

SCIENTIFIC CLASSIFICATION

The science of naming and classifying animals, plants, and other living things is called **taxonomy**.

Domain!

Kingdom!

A system divided into levels helps scientists organize all living things based on how closely they are related.

SPIDER   LIZARD   DOG   RHINOCEROS   ZEBRA   DONKEY   HORSE

Every living thing has a place in each level of **scientific classification**.

Hey, where's the spider?

Phylum!

There are several different levels of scientific classification between the animal kingdom and an animal species.

We lost the lizard.

Class!

As you move down through the levels, organisms begin to have more and more similarities with each other.

Order!

Animals of the same order, family, and genus are more closely related.

Family!

If you move up through the levels, from order to class to phylum, animal relationships become more distant.

Genus!

But each species still shares at least one common **trait** with all the rest!

Species!

I'm a horse.

THE ANIMAL KINGDOM

When looking at all life on Earth, domains and kingdoms are the top levels in the classification system.

All animals make up a kingdom called **Animalia.**

Organisms within this kingdom can be as different as a giant blue whale...

...and a tiny ant.

No matter how different two animals might be, they are more closely related to each other than to any plants, bacteria, or fungi.

Within the kingdom of Animalia, a lion and a house cat are closely related.

You can see at once that they have many similar structures and a few noticeable differences.

If you compare organisms between kingdoms you see bigger differences.

A lion is not closely related to a dandelion.

Prr

Although they are both organisms, they live life in very different ways.

ROAR!

MEOW.

Scientists arrange the individual animals in the kingdom into many different groups called **phyla.**

sniff sniff

Phyla is the plural of **phylum.**

A phylum is a large group with many different kinds of living things in it.

Most animals in the phylum Chordata have backbones.

Animals with backbones are called **vertebrates.**

Vertebrates have an internal skeleton known as an **endoskeleton.**

You belong to the phylum Chordata because you are a vertebrate.

You share a certain structure with all the other animals in this phylum.

Remember, scientists use structures, like organ systems, bone structure, and appearance, to group similar animals.

Members of a specific phylum can also be very different.

However, they are more closely related to one another than to members of other phyla.

As members of the phylum Chordata, you share more similar body structures with a fish than with a monarch butterfly.

Because of this and other specific structures, the monarch butterfly belongs to a phylum of animals without backbones called Arthropoda.

INVERTEBRATES AND ARTHROPODS (PHYLUM)

All animals without backbones are known as **invertebrates.**

About 95 out of every 100 animals do not have backbones.

Sponges, jellyfish, clams, corals, and several groups of worms are all invertebrates.

But **arthropods** are by far the largest group of invertebrates.

There are more arthropods in total on Earth than all of the other animals put together.

In fact, arthropods outnumber humans 200 million to one!

Arthropods have jointed legs.

They have a tough outer covering called an **exoskeleton.**

The exoskeleton does not grow.

POP..

Instead, as an arthropod becomes larger, it grows a new exoskeleton and sheds the old one.

All insects are arthropods.

Arachnids, like spiders and scorpions, are arthropods, too.

Crustaceans are arthropods that live in the oceans.

Crabs, lobsters, and shrimp share certain characteristics with all other arthropods.

VERTEBRATES AND MAMMALS (CLASS)

Animals can be divided again into smaller groups called **classes**.

A class includes many living things that share more characteristics than other members of a phylum.

Bats, monkeys, whales, and human beings are all classified as mammals.

Mammals have backbones just like amphibians, birds, fish, and reptiles.

But mammals share characteristics that set them apart from other vertebrates.

Snap.

While birds grow feathers and reptiles grow scales, all mammals grow hair.

Unlike all other vertebrates, newborn mammals drink milk from their mother.

Mammals and birds are warm-blooded animals.

Warm-blooded animals keep the same body temperature no matter how the temperature changes outside.

Most amphibians, fish, and reptiles are cold-blooded animals.

They rely on outside temperatures to change their body temperature.

But, for all the similarities, there are also differences within each class.

17

CLASS AND ORDER

Scientists arrange similar animals from the same class into even smaller groupings called **orders.**

GRIZZLY BEAR   BLACK BEAR   PANDA   FOX   SQUIRREL LIZARD JELLYFISH

Remember, scientists use structures, like organ systems, bone structure, and appearance, to group similar animals.

Members grouped into an order are still very different.

However, you start to see many similar or even shared structures.

18

Humans, like you, belong to an order called primates.

Gorillas, orangutans, monkeys, tarsiers, and lemurs are all primates as well.

Most members of this order have eyes that face forward...

...grasping hands, and some have grasping feet.

Some primates even have grasping tails!

Primates are also some of the most social of all animals.

Of all primates, chimpanzees have the most structures in common with humans.

FAMILY AND GENUS

Chimpanzees and humans are grouped into a **family.**

You both belong to the family called Hominidae.

Members of a family share many characteristics.

ORDER PRIMATES

FAMILY HOMINIDAE

GENUS *HOMO* (HUMANS)

GENUS *PAN* (CHIMPANZEES)

GENUS *GORILLA* (GORILLAS)

GENUS *PONGO* (ORANGUTANS)

But just because two species are extremely similar does not mean that they were or ever will be the same.

Families are groups of closely related **genera.**

Genera is the plural of **genus.**

Humans are the only living members of their genus.

You belong to a genus named *Homo* — the Latin word for human being.

Other humans have walked Earth, but are now known only through fossils and remains.

21

SPECIES

A **species** is the basic level of scientific classification.

It describes a single kind of organism.

Members of the same species can reproduce and create offspring that can also reproduce.

Members of different species may be able to reproduce, but most likely, their offspring will be unable to reproduce.

SAY WHAT?

MALE DONKEY   MULE   FEMALE HORSE

COMMON CONFUSION

Scientists identify each species with a two-word name created by combining the genus and species names of an organism.

This is called a **scientific name.**

Scientific names use Latin and Greek words to describe the species because common names for animals may not show whether they are different species.

WACK

wip

scientific name

For example, the scientific name of the eastern spotted skunk is *Spilogale putorius*.

The eastern spotted skunk's scientific name translates as smelly, spotted weasel.

Squeak

Smelly spotted weasel

Scientific names are useful because common names can be confusing.

People may call mountain lions, "cougars," "panthers," or "pumas" when referring to the same species.

But all of these names could also be used to refer to other animals.

mountain lion

puma

cougar

panther

Scientists avoid any confusion between animals by using the mountain lion's unique scientific name...

...Puma concolor.

mountain lion

= Puma concolor

CLASSIFY THE ANIMAL

How would you classify me?

You've seen me move on my own.

Sounds like my kingdom is Animalia!

I don't have a hard exoskeleton but I do have an endoskeleton.

That means I'm not an invertebrate.

I'd say I'm in the Chordata phylum.

In fact, my fur is pretty soft to the touch.

Mammals are furry —
so Mammalia is my class.

Eating meat places me in
the order of Carnivora.

Can you think of any other
animals that I look like?

Members of the Canidae family have pointed muzzles,
long bushy tails, and are sometimes called the dog family.

I can't take it anymore—

—I'm *Vulpes lagopus!*

The Arctic fox!

As you learn more about other animals...

...you can learn more about yourself and your place in the world of taxonomy.

Kingdom Animalia

Phylum Chordata

Class Mammalia

Order Carnivora

Family Canidae

Genus *Vulpes*

Species *Vulpes lagopus* (Arctic fox)

Some people remember the levels of scientific classification with a special sentence like this:

Krista Put Candy Out For Ghastly Spooks.

The starting letter of each word is also the starting letter of each level of classification.

Try to come up with your own!

That way no matter where you are, you will remember how to classify an animal!

GLOSSARY

animal kingdom (Animalia)
a kingdom made up of living things that get their energy by eating other living things.

arthropod a class of animals that share characteristics such as jointed legs and an exoskeleton.

cell the basic unit of all living things.

class a group of living things that share more characteristics than do other members of a phylum.

domain the highest level of scientific classification that holds the widest grouping of living things.

endoskeleton the internal skeleton in a vertebrate.

exoskeleton a tough outer covering that protects the body.

family a group of living things that are even more alike than those in an order.

genus; genera a smaller group of living things that are very similar but can not mate with one another; more than one genus.

invertebrate an animal without a backbone.

kingdom the second highest level of scientific classification that holds a wide grouping of living things, such as all animals or all plants.

mammal a class of animals that has a backbone, grows hair, and feeds its young on the mother's milk.

order a group of living things that are more alike than those in a class.

organ systems a group of organs that work together to help the body function.

organism any living thing.

phylum; phyla a large group of many different kinds of living things that are more alike than those in a kingdom; more than one phylum.

scientific classification a leveled system by which scientists arrange living things into many groups.

scientific name a special two-word name, created by combining the genus and species names, used to identify each individual organism.

species the basic level of scientific classification made up of closely related living things with many similarities.

structure a body part of a living thing.

taxonomy the science of naming and classifying living things.

trait a physical or behavioral characteristic.

vertebrate an animal with a backbone.

FIND OUT MORE

Books

The Animal Book: A Visual Encyclopedia of Life on Earth
by David Burnie
(DK Publishing, 2013)

Animal Classification
by Jenny Fretland VanVoorst
(ABDO, 2014)

Animal Encyclopedia: 2,500 Animals with Photos, Maps, and More!
by Dr. Lucy Spelman
(National Geographic, 2012)

Animals: Mammals, Birds, Reptiles, Amphibians, Fish, and Other Animals
by Shar Levine and Leslie Johnstone
(Crabtree, 2010)

Super Nature Encyclopedia
by Derek Harvey
(DK Publishing, 2012)

Ultimate Bugopedia: The Most Complete Bug Reference Ever
by Darlyne Murawski and Nancy Honovich
(National Geographic, 2013)

Wild World: An Encyclopedia of Animals
by Jinny Johnson
(Millbrook, 2013)

Websites

BBC Nature: Animals
http://www.bbc.co.uk/nature/animals
Watch thousands of short wildlife videos that identify and discuss hundreds of species of animals.

BBC Bitesize Science: Variation
http://www.bbc.co.uk/bitesize/ks2 /science/living_things/variation/read/1/
Read about the similarities and differences among plants, and then play a clickable game to classify animals into different groups.

National Geographic Kids: Creature Features
http://kids.nationalgeographic.com/kids /animals/creaturefeature/
Select an animal to watch a video or hear its call, or read an article to learn more about its unique characteristics.

Natural Museum of History: Carl Linnaeus
http://www.nhm.ac.uk/nature-online /science-of-natural-history/biographies /linnaeus/index.html
Meet Carl Linnaeus—the influential scientist who developed scientific classification!

Nova: Classifying Life
http://www.pbs.org/wgbh/nova/nature /classifying-life.html
Learn more about the classification system as you play a game to classify a bear, an orchid, and a sea cucumber.

PBS Teachers: Animal Classification Game
http://www.pbslearningmedia.org/asset /lsps07_int_animalclass/
Read quick classification facts and then play a short game to test your knowledge.

San Diego Zoo Kids: Games
http://kids.sandiegozoo.org/games/
Meet your favorite zoo animals through a variety of activities including drawing, games, and crafts.

Scholastic Teachers: Science Study Jams!
http://studyjams.scholastic.com /studyjams/jams/science/index.htm
All of your questions about plant and animal life will be answered in clickable lessons featuring narrated slideshows, key terms, and short quizzes.

INDEX

www.ingramcontent.com/pod-product-compliance
Lightning Source LLC
LaVergne TN
LVHW070840080426
835513LV00023B/2417